God Powered Journal:

Unlock Your Inner Superhero in 30 Days

Tina Brinkley Potts LLC

386 Walmart Drive, Suite 7 #39, Camden, DE 19934
inquiries@tinabrinkleypotts.com
302-208-8844

The contents of this book are intended for general informational and educational purposes only. The ideas, concepts, and techniques presented in this book are based on the author's personal experiences and perspectives.

Readers are advised to consult with appropriate professionals before implementing any strategies or making decisions based on the content of this book, especially if dealing with mental health, financial, or other significant life issues. The author and the publisher do not assume responsibility for any consequences or adverse effects resulting directly or indirectly from the use of information contained in this book.

The content is not intended to substitute for professional advice, diagnosis, or treatment. Always seek the advice of your qualified mental health provider, financial advisor, or other relevant professional with any questions you may have regarding a medical condition, mental health, or your financial situation.

The author and the publisher disclaim any liability or responsibility for any loss or damage incurred by readers as a result of applying the information presented in this book. The views expressed in this book are those of the author and do not necessarily reflect the views of the publisher. The book is not intended to be a substitute for independent professional advice.

Day 1

I am worthy of love and acceptance just as I am.

I am grateful for

♡ _______________________________________ ♡
♡ _______________________________________ ♡
♡ _______________________________________ ♡

Self-Care

Take a relaxing bubble bath with scented candles and soothing music.

Goal getta

Set a goal to read a certain number of books or explore a specific genre within the next 30 days.

Mindful Eating

Pay attention to your hunger and fullness cues before, during, and after each meal.

Random acts of kindness

Send a handwritten thank-you note to someone who has made a difference in your life.

Digital detox

Designate specific times of the day to be technology-free, such as during meals or before bed.

Write about three things you are grateful for in your life right now.

Physical activity

Go for a brisk walk or jog around your neighborhood.

Personal growth

Set a timer for 15 minutes. Write down all of your thoughts without judgment. Decide if they are thoughts you want.

Day 2

I choose to embrace my unique qualities and celebrate my individuality.

I am grateful for

♡ ____ ♡
♡ ____ ♡
♡ ____ ♡

Self-Care

Treat yourself to a professional massage or indulge in a self-massage using essential oils.

Goal getta

Establish a daily meditation or mindfulness practice and set a goal to meditate for a certain amount of time each day.

Mindful Eating

Eat slowly and savor each bite, noticing the flavors, textures, and aromas of your food.

Random acts of kindness

Hold the door open for someone and greet them with a smile.

Digital detox

Turn off notifications on your phone to minimize distractions.

Reflect on a person who has had a positive impact on your life and express gratitude for their presence.

____
____
____
____
____
____
____
____
____
____
____
____
____

Physical activity

Take a dance class or join a dance fitness program.

Personal growth

Think of the last person/situation you gossiped about. Now, spend a few minutes sending that person compassion and joy.

Day 3

I am deserving of happiness, success, and fulfillment.

I am grateful for

♡ ____ ♡
♡ ____ ♡
♡ ____ ♡

Self-Care

Spend a day unplugged from technology and enjoy activities like reading a book or taking a nature walk.

Goal getta

Set a fitness goal, such as completing a specific number of workouts or achieving a personal best in a particular exercise.

Mindful Eating

Engage your senses by appreciating the visual presentation of your meal.

Random acts of kindness

Offer to help a neighbor with a task or chore they may need assistance with.

Digital detox

Go for a walk or engage in outdoor activities without your phone.

Write about a happy memory that brings you joy and gratitude.

Physical activity

Try a new workout routine, such as HIIT (High-Intensity Interval Training) or Pilates.

Personal growth

Think of 1 thing that isn't going exactly as planned. Take 5 minutes to visualize it exactly as you want it to go.

Day 4

I release all self-doubt and trust in my ability to overcome any challenges.

I am grateful for

♡ ____ ♡
♡ ____ ♡
♡ ____ ♡

Self-Care

Practice deep breathing exercises or meditation to calm your mind and promote relaxation.

Goal getta

Set a goal to learn a new skill or hobby, like playing a musical instrument, painting, or cooking a new recipe.

Mindful Eating

Express gratitude for the nourishment your food provides before taking the first bite.

Random acts of kindness

Leave a generous tip for a service worker who has provided excellent service.

Digital detox

Dedicate one day a week as a screen-free day.

Physical activity

Take a bike ride in a local park or explore a new cycling trail.

Personal growth

Create a vision board to visualize your goals and aspirations.

Day 5

I am resilient and capable of adapting to any situation that comes my way.

I am grateful for

♡ ____ ♡
♡ ____ ♡
♡ ____ ♡

Self-Care

Have a movie night at home with your favorite films or TV shows, complete with cozy blankets and snacks.

Goal getta

Set a goal to practice gratitude daily by writing down three things you are grateful for each day.

Mindful Eating

Chew your food thoroughly and focus on the act of chewing.

Random acts of kindness

Donate gently used clothing or household items to a local shelter or charity.

Digital detox

Establish a "no screens in the bedroom" rule to promote better sleep.

Physical activity

Attend a group fitness class, such as Zumba, yoga, or kickboxing.

Personal growth

Today, as stressful situations come up, don't react. Instead, practice heart breathing for 5 minutes.

Day 6

I love and accept myself unconditionally, flaws and all.

I am grateful for

♡ _______________________ ♡
♡ _______________________ ♡
♡ _______________________ ♡

Self-Care

Engage in a creative activity like painting, drawing, or crafting.

Goal getta

Set a goal to establish a morning routine that includes activities like meditation, exercise, journaling, or reading.

Mindful Eating

Put your fork down between bites to slow down the pace of your meal.

Random acts of kindness

Offer to babysit for a friend or family member, giving them some time for themselves.

Digital detox

Engage in hobbies or activities that don't involve screens, such as painting, gardening, or playing a musical instrument.

Reflect on a difficult situation you've overcome and express gratitude for the lessons learned.

Physical activity

Go hiking and enjoy the beauty of nature.

Personal growth

Take a few moment and practice projecting love to inanimate objects. Start with the doorknob, then the a light switch on the wall.

Day 7

I am enough, exactly as I am in this moment.

I am grateful for

♡ _______________________________ ♡
♡ _______________________________ ♡
♡ _______________________________ ♡

Self-Care

Practice yoga or try out a new exercise routine that you enjoy.

Goal getta

Set a goal to declutter and organize a specific area of your living space within the next 30 days.

Mindful Eating

Take a moment to breathe and relax before starting your meal.

Random acts of kindness

Leave uplifting and positive sticky notes in public places for strangers to find.

Digital detox

Read a physical book instead of using an e-reader or reading on a screen.

Write about a place or location that brings you peace and gratitude.

____

____

____

____

____

____

____

____

____

____

____

____

____

____

Physical activity

Swim laps at a local pool or take a water aerobics class.

Personal growth

For 5 minutes, practice this breathing/sound exercise: Breathe in deep through the nose, and exhale through the mouth saying "AHHHH"

Day 8

I choose to focus on my strengths and build upon them.

I am grateful for

Self-Care

Get a good night's sleep by establishing a bedtime routine and ensuring a peaceful sleep environment.

Goal getta

Set a goal to practice a specific self-care activity, like taking a relaxing bath, going for a walk in nature, or practicing yoga, for a certain number of days.

Mindful Eating

Notice the sensations of hunger and how they change as you eat.

Random acts of kindness

Compliment a stranger sincerely and genuinely.

Digital detox

Plan a day trip or weekend getaway to a location without Wi-Fi or cellular service.

Physical activity

Play a sport with friends, such as basketball, soccer, or tennis.

Personal growth

Take up a new hobby or revisit an old one that brings you joy.

Day 9

I am worthy of self-care and prioritize my well-being.

I am grateful for

♡ ____ ♡
♡ ____ ♡
♡ ____ ♡

Self-Care

amper yourself with a DIY spa day
at home, including face masks,
manicures, and pedicures.

Goal getta

Set a goal to save a specific amount
of money within the next 30 days
by implementing a budget or
reducing unnecessary expenses.

Mindful Eating

Avoid distractions like screens or multitasking while eating and focus
solely on your meal.

Random acts of kindness

Volunteer at a local charity or organization that aligns with your
interests or values.

Digital detox

Have a device-free meal with family or friends, focusing on quality
conversations.

Write about a book, movie, or song that has inspired you and express gratitude for its impact on your life.

Physical activity

Try a new outdoor activity, like kayaking, paddleboarding, or rock climbing.

Personal growth

Send love to an enemy. Spend 5 minutes writing to them with compassion. Then burn it.

Day 10

I am worthy of pursuing my dreams and turning them into reality.

I am grateful for

Self-Care

Go for a nature walk or hike to connect with the outdoors and enjoy the benefits of fresh air and sunshine.

Goal getta

Set a goal to establish a regular writing practice, whether it's journaling, starting a blog, or working on a creative writing project.

Mindful Eating

Practice portion control by serving yourself a reasonable amount of food.

Random acts of kindness

Offer to walk a friend's or neighbor's dog.

Digital detox

Practice mindfulness or meditation without using any digital apps or guided sessions.

Physical activity

Take a yoga or meditation class to improve flexibility and mindfulness.

Personal growth

Identify a limiting belief you've been telling yourself. How can you process it up?

Day 11

I am confident in my abilities and trust in my intuition.

I am grateful for

Self-Care

Treat yourself to a delicious and nutritious meal or try out a new recipe.

Goal getta

Set a goal to develop a new healthy habit, such as drinking more water, eating more vegetables, or getting enough sleep.

Mindful Eating

Take note of the ingredients and appreciate the effort and care that went into preparing your meal.

Random acts of kindness

Send a care package or handwritten note to a member of the military serving overseas.

Digital detox

Write in a journal or practice free writing to express your thoughts and emotions.

Write about a recent accomplishment or milestone you've achieved and express gratitude for the journey.

____
____
____
____
____
____
____
____
____
____
____
____
____

Physical activity

Join a recreational sports league in your community.

Personal growth

Today, each time you find yourself upset, say your crazy expression. Pattern interrupt

Day 12

I deserve to set healthy boundaries that honor my needs and values.

I am grateful for

♡ _______________________________________ ♡
♡ _______________________________________ ♡
♡ _______________________________________ ♡

Self-Care

Practice mindfulness by engaging in activities like journaling, coloring, or practicing gratitude.

Goal getta

Set a goal to connect with loved ones more frequently, whether it's scheduling regular phone calls, meetups, or video chats.

Mindful Eating

Consider the source of your food and its impact on the environment.

Random acts of kindness

Buy extra groceries and donate them to a food bank or a family in need.

Digital detox

Explore new recipes and cook a meal without relying on digital recipes.

Express gratitude for the simple pleasures in life, like a warm cup of coffee, a good laugh, or a cozy blanket.

Physical activity

Go for a refreshing swim in the ocean, lake, or river.

Personal growth

Develop a reframe for your greatest challenge today.

Day 13

I choose to let go of past mistakes and embrace new opportunities for growth.

I am grateful for

____

____

____

Self-Care

Schedule a social activity with friends or loved ones, such as a coffee date, picnic, or game night.

Goal getta

Set a goal to learn about a specific topic or area of interest by reading books, watching documentaries, or taking online courses.

Mindful Eating

Observe any emotional or psychological connections you have with food and how it affects your eating habits.

Random acts of kindness

Offer to help an elderly person with their groceries or household chores.

Digital detox

Have a digital declutter session by organizing and deleting unnecessary files, emails, or apps.

____
____
____
____
____
____
____
____
____
____
____
____
____
____

Physical activity

Take a group fitness class outdoors, such as boot camp or outdoor yoga.

Personal growth

Practice Segment Intending throughout today.

Day 14

I am grateful for my body and treat it with kindness and respect.

I am grateful for

♡ ___________________________ ♡
♡ ___________________________ ♡
♡ ___________________________ ♡

Self-Care

Listen to your favorite music or create a playlist that uplifts your mood.

Goal getta

Set a goal to volunteer or give back to your community by participating in a local charity or organizing a community service project.

Mindful Eating

Be curious about the nutritional value of your food and how it benefits your body.

Random acts of kindness

Leave a kind and encouraging comment on someone's social media post.

Digital detox

Take up a new hobby or craft that doesn't require digital devices, such as knitting, woodworking, or painting.

____
____
____
____
____
____
____
____
____
____
____
____

Physical activity

Practice strength training exercises using weights or resistance bands.

Personal growth

As you go throughout your day, if someone gossips, reframe the conversation

Day 15

I am grateful for my body and treat it with kindness and respect.

I am grateful for

♡ ____ ♡
♡ ____ ♡
♡ ____ ♡

Self-Care

ngage in a mindful eating practice
y savoring each bite and focusing
n the flavors and textures of your
food.

Goal getta

Set a goal to practice a specific form
of self-reflection or introspection, such
as daily journal prompts or regular
moments of self-assessment.

Mindful Eating

Experiment with new flavors and cuisines to expand your palate and
cultivate a sense of adventure.

Random acts of kindness

Bake homemade treats and share them with your coworkers or
neighbors.

Digital detox

Engage in physical activities, like exercising, yoga, or dancing, without
following along with a digital instructor.

Physical activity

Sign up for a local charity walk or run to support a cause you care about.

Personal growth

As you go through your day, if someone starts a conversation that is negative, reframe it.

Day 16

I am capable of achieving anything I set my mind to.

I am grateful for

♡ ______________________________ ♡
♡ ______________________________ ♡
♡ ______________________________ ♡

Self-Care

Declutter and organize a space in your home that brings you peace and a sense of order.

Goal getta

Set a goal to establish a consistent exercise routine, whether it's going to the gym, practicing yoga, or engaging in home workouts.

Mindful Eating

Practice gratitude for the farmers, growers, and everyone involved in bringing food to your table.

Random acts of kindness

Offer to drive someone who may not have access to transportation to their appointment or errands.

Digital detox

Spend quality time with loved ones, engaging in activities or conversations without digital distractions.

Reflect on a challenge or setback you've faced and express gratitude for the strength and resilience it has built within you.

____
____
____
____
____
____
____
____
____
____
____
____
____
____

Physical activity

Explore a new hiking trail or nature reserve in your area.

Personal growth

Focus, Pocus, Focus: Focus on doing 1 thing for an hour. If anything else comes to you, write it down but go back to the 1 thing. Stay focused!

Day 17

I am open to receiving abundance and opportunities that come my way.

I am grateful for

♡ _______________________________ ♡
♡ _______________________________ ♡
♡ _______________________________ ♡

Self-Care

Spend quality time with a beloved pet or consider volunteering at an animal shelter.

Goal getta

Set a goal to develop a better work-life balance by implementing specific boundaries and creating dedicated time for relaxation and leisure activities.

Mindful Eating

Engage in mindful grocery shopping by selecting fresh, whole foods and being aware of your choices.

Random acts of kindness

Plant a tree or flowers in a public space to beautify the environment.

Digital detox

Create art or do crafts using traditional materials, like paints, clay, or paper.

Write about a friend who has been there for you during difficult times and express gratitude for their friendship.

____

Physical activity

Try a new workout video or fitness app for a guided workout at home.

Personal growth

Practice I AM affirmations.

Day 18

I forgive myself for any past mistakes and allow myself to move forward.

I am grateful for

♡ _______________________________ ♡
♡ _______________________________ ♡
♡ _______________________________ ♡

Self-Care

Take a leisurely nature drive to enjoy scenic views and explore new areas.

Goal getta

Set a goal to improve your productivity by adopting time management techniques or breaking down larger tasks into smaller, manageable steps.

Mindful Eating

Eat with gratitude for the cultural and culinary traditions that have shaped your meals.

Random acts of kindness

Offer to tutor or mentor a student who may be struggling academically.

Digital detox

Play board games or card games with family or friends instead of relying on digital entertainment.

Physical activity

Take a martial arts class to learn self-defense techniques and improve discipline.

Personal growth

Practice YOU ARE affirmations

Day 19

I am grateful for

♡ ______________________________________ ♡
♡ ______________________________________ ♡
♡ ______________________________________ ♡

Self-Care

Write in a journal to reflect on your thoughts, feelings, and goals.

Goal getta

Set a goal to explore new opportunities for personal growth, such as attending workshops, networking events, or joining a new club or group.

Mindful Eating

Listen to your body's cues of satiety and stop eating when you feel comfortably full.

Random acts of kindness

Leave a thank-you note or small gift for your mail carrier or delivery person.

Digital detox

Volunteer or participate in community service activities that don't involve technology.

Take a dance break and have a mini dance party in your living room.

Take a situation that isn't going quite the way you want and do the Speak Life Exercise

Day 20

I trust in my journey and have faith in the process of life.

I am grateful for

♡ ____ ♡
♡ ____ ♡
♡ ____ ♡

Self-Care

Treat yourself to a new book or indulge in reading your favorite genre.

Goal getta

Set a goal to practice a specific form of creativity, such as writing, painting, photography, or playing a musical instrument, for a designated amount of time each day.

Mindful Eating

Acknowledge any feelings of guilt or judgment that may arise around certain foods and work towards self-compassion.

Random acts of kindness

Write positive reviews for local businesses you appreciate and frequent.

Digital detox

Take a digital detox retreat or join a technology-free workshop or retreat.

____
____
____
____
____
____
____
____
____
____
____
____
____
____

Physical activity

Go for a scenic jog or walk in a nearby park or botanical garden.

Personal growth

Reflect on your strengths and Passions with the "Language" Framework

Day 21

I choose to surround myself with positive and uplifting influences.

I am grateful for

Self-Care

Engage in a physical activity that you enjoy, such as dancing, playing a sport, or going for a swim

Goal getta

Set a goal to practice self-compassion and self-love by engaging in positive affirmations, self-care activities, and cultivating a positive mindset.

Mindful Eating

Practice mindful snacking by choosing nourishing options and being aware of portion sizes.

Random acts of kindness

Offer to mow a neighbor's lawn or shovel their driveway.

Digital detox

Practice gratitude by writing down three things you're grateful for each day, without using digital devices.

Express gratitude for your senses—the ability to see, hear, taste, touch, and smell the world around you.

____
____
____
____
____
____
____
____
____
____
____
____
____
____

Physical activity

Try a new team sport, like volleyball, softball, or flag football.

Personal growth

Think of a way you are not speaking your truth. Process it up

Day 22

am proud of my progress and celebrate my achievements, no matter how small.

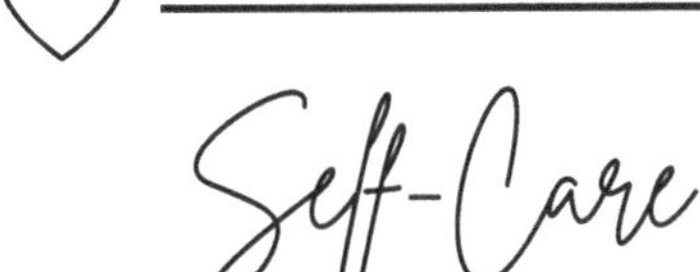

I am grateful for

♡ ______________________________________ ♡
♡ ______________________________________ ♡
♡ ______________________________________ ♡

Self-Care

Practice mindfulness or relaxation exercises before bedtime to promote a restful night's sleep.

Goal getta

Set a goal to establish a healthier sleep routine by prioritizing consistent bedtimes and creating a relaxing evening routine.

Mindful Eating

Experiment with mindful cooking or meal preparation, focusing on each step of the process.

Random acts of kindness

Surprise a friend or family member with their favorite homemade meal or treat.

Digital detox

Explore nature and go for a hike or walk in a park, leaving your phone behind or in airplane mode.

Write about a positive change or transformation you've experienced in your life and express gratitude for the journey.

____
____
____
____
____
____
____
____
____
____
____
____
____
____

Physical activity

Take a high-energy fitness class, like spin cycling or aerobics.

Personal growth

Break up your routine. If you go to work, take a different route today. Pattern Interrupt

Day 23

I release the need to compare myself to others and focus on my own growth.

I am grateful for

♡ ____ ♡
♡ ____ ♡
♡ ____ ♡

Self-Care

Take yourself out on a date to a museum, art gallery, or any other place that sparks your interest.

Goal getta

Set a goal to improve your communication skills by practicing active listening, expressing yourself clearly, or seeking opportunities for public speaking.

Mindful Eating

Reflect on the source and quality of the ingredients in your meals and how they contribute to your overall well-being.

Random acts of kindness

Donate books or educational materials to a local school or library.

Digital detox

Engage in self-reflection or journaling sessions to gain clarity and insight into your thoughts and emotions.

Reflect on a favorite hobby or activity that brings you joy and express gratitude for the opportunity to engage in it.

Physical activity

Participate in a virtual fitness challenge or race.

Personal growth

Practice self love in the mirror. Say 25 statements to yourself honoring all experiences that has happened in the last month, even the difficult experiences.

Day 24

I am worthy of self-expression and speaking my truth.

I am grateful for

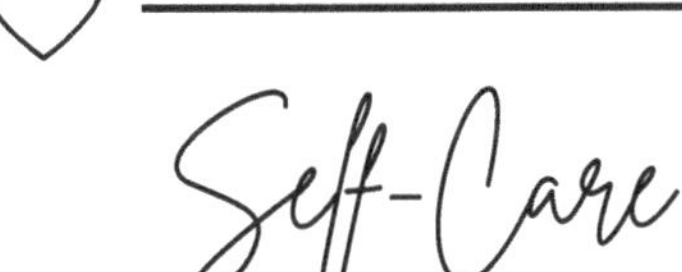

Self-Care

Cook or bake a special treat for yourself, indulging in the joy of creating something delicious.

Goal getta

Set a goal to learn a new language or improve your proficiency in a language you are already studying.

Mindful Eating

Notice any emotional or environmental triggers that may lead to mindless eating and find alternative ways to address them.

Random acts of kindness

Offer to pick up groceries or run errands for someone who may have difficulty doing so themselves.

Digital detox

Write letters or cards to friends or family members instead of sending digital messages.

____

____

____

____

____

____

____

____

____

____

____

____

____

____

Physical activity

Engage in interval training by alternating between bursts of high-intensity exercise and rest.

Personal growth

Before you go to sleep, practice sending love to the doorknob, the light fixture. Now send the love to the relationship that is troubled.

Day 25

I choose to let go of negative self-talk and replace it with empowering words.

I am grateful for

♡ ______________________________ ♡
♡ ______________________________ ♡
♡ ______________________________ ♡

Self-Care

Spend time in nature by having a picnic, meditating outdoors, or simply enjoying the beauty of your surroundings.

Goal getta

Set a goal to reduce stress and increase mindfulness by implementing a daily relaxation practice, like deep breathing exercises or guided meditation.

Mindful Eating

Pause midway through your meal to assess your satisfaction level and adjust your eating pace accordingly.

Random acts of kindness

Volunteer your time at a local animal shelter or rescue organization.

Digital detox

Spend time in a quiet and technology-free space to reflect, relax, and recharge.

Write about a valuable life lesson you've learned from a mistake or failure and express gratitude for the growth it has provided.

____
____
____
____
____
____
____
____
____
____
____
____
____
____

Physical activity

Go for a power walk during your lunch break to boost energy and clear your mind.

Personal growth

Practice active listening and empathetic communication in your interactions with others.

Day 26

I am grateful for the lessons I've learned and the wisdom I've gained.

I am grateful for

♡ ____ ♡
♡ ____ ♡
♡ ____ ♡

Self-Care

Learn a new skill or hobby that you've always wanted to explore, such as playing a musical instrument or learning a new language.

Goal getta

Set a goal to explore a new hobby or interest, such as gardening, cooking, dancing, or photography.

Mindful Eating

Be mindful of your body's response to different foods, noting any sensitivities or reactions.

Random acts of kindness

Offer to teach someone a skill or hobby that you excel at.

Digital detox

Explore new areas of interest by reading physical magazines or visiting a local library.

Physical activity

Practice yoga or stretching exercises to improve flexibility and relieve tension.

Personal growth

Learn about a different culture or tradition to foster cultural understanding.

Day 27

I am deserving of self-compassion and practice kindness towards myself.

I am grateful for

Self-Care

ake a break from your routine and have a self-care day filled with activities that bring you joy, relaxation, and rejuvenation.

Goal getta

Set a goal to establish a regular gratitude practice by writing thank-you notes, expressing appreciation to others, or keeping a gratitude journal.

Mindful Eating

Practice gratitude for the connections and social interactions that come with sharing meals with others.

Random acts of kindness

Leave a generous tip for a server at a restaurant.

Digital detox

Engage in puzzles or brain-teasers, like crosswords or Sudoku, instead of relying on digital versions.

Express gratitude for the opportunities for education and personal growth that you have access to.

Physical activity

Incorporate a daily 15-minute workout routine into your schedule.

Personal growth

Engage in activities that challenge your comfort zone and help you overcome fears.

Day 28

I am confident in my abilities to overcome obstacles and create positive change.

I am grateful for

♡ _______________________ ♡
♡ _______________________ ♡
♡ _______________________ ♡

Self-Care

Practice self-compassion by speaking kindly to yourself and engaging in positive self-talk.

Goal getta

Set a goal to improve your physical well-being by adopting a healthier diet, reducing sugar intake, or drinking more water.

Mindful Eating

Take a moment to appreciate the effort you put into nourishing your body through mindful eating.

Random acts of kindness

Send a small gift or care package to a friend or family member who may be going through a tough time.

Digital detox

Practice self-care activities, such as taking a bath, practicing aromatherapy, or doing a face mask, without any digital distractions.

Physical activity

Take a dance-inspired workout class, such as barre or hip-hop dance.

Personal growth

Day 29

am a work in progress, and each day, I become a better version of myself.

I am grateful for

♡ ____ ♡
♡ ____ ♡
♡ ____ ♡

Self-Care

Explore a new park or garden in your area and spend time connecting with nature.

Goal getta

Set a goal to engage in regular acts of kindness and contribute to making a positive impact in the lives of others.

Mindful Eating

Reflect on the impact of food waste and consider ways to reduce it through mindful meal planning and storage.

Random acts of kindness

Offer to help a parent or caregiver with childcare for a few hours.

Digital detox

Engage in outdoor activities, like gardening, bird-watching, or stargazing, without using digital devices.

Physical activity

Join a recreational sports club or group to meet new people and stay active.

Personal growth

Identify limiting beliefs and work on replacing them with empowering beliefs.

Day 30

I am loved, supported, and worthy of all the good that life has to offer.

I am grateful for

♡ ________________________________ ♡
♡ ________________________________ ♡
♡ ________________________________ ♡

Self-Care

Engage in a digital detox by taking a break from social media and enjoying uninterrupted time for yourself.

Goal getta

Set a goal to challenge yourself by stepping out of your comfort zone and try something new, whether it's a new sport, a new style of clothing, or a new type of cuisine.

Mindful Eating

Embrace non-judgment and cultivate a compassionate attitude towards yourself and your relationship with food.

Random acts of kindness

Simply smile and say hello to strangers as you go about your day, spreading positivity.

Digital detox

Connect with nature by practicing grounding techniques, like walking barefoot on grass or sand, without any digital distractions.

Express gratitude for the journey of self-discovery and personal growth you are embarking on.

Physical activity

Have a friendly competition with friends or family, such as a game of frisbee or mini-golf.

Personal growth

Reflect on your accomplishments and celebrate your successes, no matter how small.